EXPLORE CHINA

A *Mulan* Discovery Book

By Charlotte Cheng

Special thanks to Nina Duthie,
UCLA Department of Asian Languages and Cultures

Lerner Publications • Minneapolis

Lerner Publications Company
An imprint of Lerner Publishing Group, Inc.
241 First Avenue North
Minneapolis, MN 55401 USA

For reading levels and more information, look up this
title at www.lernerbooks.com.

Main body text set in Mikado 12/20.
Typeface provided by HVD Fonts.

Library of Congress Cataloging-in-Publication Data

The Cataloging-in-Publication Data for *Explore
China: A Mulan Discovery Book* is on file at the
Library of Congress.
ISBN 978-1-5415-5491-7 (lib. bdg.)
ISBN 978-1-5415-7389-5 (pbk.)
ISBN 978-1-5415-6142-7 (eb pdf)

Manufactured in the United States of America
1-45809-42691-3/28/2019

CONTENTS

Welcome to China   4

Chinese Dynasties   6

The Great Wall   8

Imperial Cities   10

Daily Life in Ancient China   12

Clothing   14

Jewelry and Accessories   16

Honoring the Ancestors   18

Joining the Army   20

Army Life   22

Animal Symbols   24

Food and Drink   26

Chinese Writing   28

Traditional Chinese Art   30

China's Geography   32

Chinese Inventions   34

Music and Dance   36

Martial Arts   38

Celebrations and Festivals   40

Welcome Home   42

Glossary   44

Index   46

WELCOME TO CHINA

Mulan's homeland is rich with history, art, and legends. Let's explore China's **culture** and history together!

A Land with a Long History

China is a country located on the continent of **Asia**. One of the world's oldest **civilizations**, Chinese society is responsible for many important inventions and discoveries. Today, over 1.3 billion people live in China. It has the largest population of any country in the world.

China

Meet the Legend

Mulan is an important heroine in Chinese culture because of her courage and honor. Historians think her story was first written by an unknown poet over 1,400 years ago. The story tells of a woman who disguises herself as a man and goes to battle in her father's place. She fights so bravely that she is honored by the emperor. Even today, Mulan remains a popular and respected figure.

From Poem to Film

The legend of Mulan has been retold and reimagined many times. In 1998, Disney released the animated film *Mulan*. The filmmakers drew inspiration from different periods in China's history. In this book, you'll discover aspects of Chinese history and culture that inspired the film. You'll learn about life in ancient China and the achievements of the Chinese people.

CHINESE DYNASTIES

The history of China spans thousands of years. From about 1600 BCE to 1912 CE, different families ruled China at different times. These ruling families were called **dynasties**, and the ruler of China was called the **emperor**.

Ruling Families

Many Chinese dynasties lasted hundreds of years. Others, like the Qin dynasty, did not last long at all. The filmmakers who worked on the *Mulan* movie were particularly inspired by the Han and Tang dynasties.

Major Chinese Dynasties	
Shang Dynasty (about 1600-1046 BCE)	Tang Dynasty (618-907 CE)
Zhou Dynasty (1046-256 BCE)	Five Dynasties and Ten Kingdoms (907-960 CE)
Qin Dynasty (221-206 BCE)	Song Dynasty (960-1279 CE)
Han Dynasty (206 BCE-220 CE)	Yuan Dynasty (1279-1368 CE)
Six Dynasties (220-581 CE)	Ming Dynasty (1368-1644 CE)
Sui Dynasty (581-618 CE)	Qing Dynasty (1644-1912 CE)

Common Era, or CE, begins at year 1 of the **Gregorian calendar**. This is the most widely used calendar in the world today. **Before the Common Era**, or BCE, refers to dates before year 1 CE. An event in 1000 BCE took place one thousand years before 1 CE.

Han Dynasty

During the Han dynasty, education was highly valued. An imperial academy was established in 124 BCE. The school taught and trained people to become government officials. Paper and porcelain were invented during this dynasty. Trade routes that would one day connect China to the Mediterranean Sea also began to develop. These routes became known as the **Silk Road**.

A Han emperor meeting with scholars

Tang Dynasty

Known as a golden age, the Tang dynasty was a time of peace and prosperity. Trade flourished along the Silk Road. The Chinese traded silk, spices, tea, and other valuable items with Central Asian and some European countries. Literature, especially poetry, also thrived. Over fifty thousand poems written during this period survive to the present. Some Tang inventions include paper money, printed books, gunpowder, and mechanical clocks.

Painting of a Tang dynasty poet

THE GREAT WALL

The *Mulan* animated film begins with a scene at the **Great Wall** of China. The Huns, **nomadic** tribes from the north, are invading China's border. Their leader, Shan-Yu, is a fearsome warrior. The guards at the wall light signal fires to alert the kingdom of the attack.

Defense Against Invaders

Shan-Yu is a fictional character, but threats of invasion in China's history were real. The Great Wall was originally built to prevent northern tribes from invading China. Workers used stone, brick, earth, and wood to build the structure. **Watchtowers** and **garrisons** were built along the wall to help guard the border.

Across the Dynasties

The idea to build the Great Wall came from Qin Shi Huang. He was the first emperor of the Qin dynasty (221–206 BCE). Existing structures and new construction were linked together to form the wall. About 1,500 miles (2,414 km) of the wall were built during this period. The size and length of the wall changed over the centuries. Different dynasties extended, strengthened, and rebuilt the wall. At times, parts of the wall reached from China's western border all the way to the Pacific Ocean!

Still Standing

The Great Wall that still stands today was mostly built during the Ming dynasty (1368–1644 CE). It stretches for about 5,500 miles (8,850 km). This impressive structure is considered a national symbol of China.

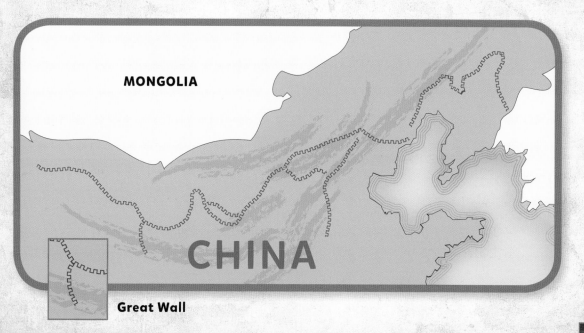

MONGOLIA

CHINA

Great Wall

IMPERIAL CITIES

The Emperor rules China from the Imperial Palace, located in the country's **capital**. When he hears of the Huns' invasion, he commands the Imperial Army to recruit more soldiers.

Ancient Capitals

The Four Great Ancient Capitals of China are Beijing, Nanjing, Luoyang, and Xi'an. Luoyang and Xi'an were capitals during the Han and Tang dynasties. There are many ancient temples and buildings still standing in these cities.

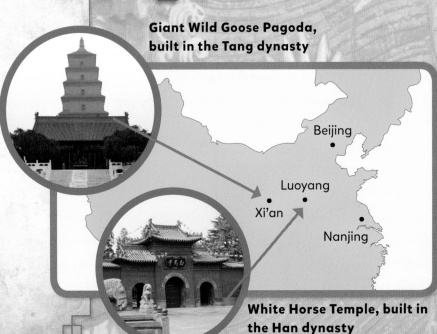

Giant Wild Goose Pagoda, built in the Tang dynasty

Beijing

Luoyang

Xi'an

Nanjing

White Horse Temple, built in the Han dynasty

The Forbidden City

Imperial Palace, Beijing

Starting in 1420 CE, the emperor lived and ruled in the Forbidden City. Located in Beijing, the palace was forbidden to commoners. Only select people were allowed to visit. The Forbidden City was made up of 980 buildings where government officials lived. The officials helped the emperor make important decisions.

Beijing Today

China has not been ruled by an emperor since the Qing dynasty fell in 1912 CE. The Chinese government today includes a president and a **parliament**. Government officials work in Beijing, the country's capital.

Great Hall of the People, Beijing

DAILY LIFE IN ANCIENT CHINA

Fa Mulan lives in a village far from the Imperial capital. She is a respectful daughter to her parents, Fa Zhou and Fa Li. Mulan's grandmother also lives with them.

Villages

In ancient China, most of the families who lived in villages were farmers. Grandparents, parents, and children would live together in a house. Most houses were close to a market town where people could shop and **socialize**.

Family Name and Honor

In China, a person's family name comes before the personal name. Mulan's family name is Fa, so her full name is Fa Mulan. Family is very important in Chinese society. People would practice good behavior to bring **honor** to their family. Examples include obeying parents and other elders, being respectful and kind to others, and serving the country. Respecting and obeying one's parents and ancestors is called **filial piety**.

Fa Mulan's name in Chinese

Beliefs and Values

Filial piety is one teaching of a belief system called **Confucianism**. Confucius was a teacher who lived from 551 to 479 BCE. His teachings became widely accepted during the Han dynasty. Confucius believed that society worked like a family. Just as children obeyed and respected their elders, all people had to obey and respect the emperor. Even today, Confucianism has a strong influence on Chinese society.

Statue of Confucius

CLOTHING

One way Mulan can bring honor to her family is to marry well. She dresses in formal clothing to meet the town's matchmaker. Traditional Chinese clothing differed in style, material, and even color, depending on a person's status.

Hanfu

Traditional Chinese clothing is called **Hanfu**. The term translates to "clothing of the Han people." However, it can refer to traditional clothes from many dynasties. Hanfu typically includes a shirt that crosses in front, a skirt or pants, and a belt or sash. Shoes were usually made of black cloth.

shirt

sash

long shirt

waist skirt

skirt

shoe

pants

sock

A Sign of Status

People on farms and villages wore clothes made from cotton, linen, or hemp fibers. Only the wealthy could afford clothes made from **silk**. Silk is a soft and light fabric made from the cocoons of silkworms.

Silkworms and cocoons

Dress for the Occasion

Hanfu costume

Villagers wore comfortable homemade clothes when they worked. People might wear clothes with better-quality fabrics in different colors to attend formal events. These could include festivals, ceremonies, and important meetings. Upper-class women might wear Hanfu with wide sleeves and flowing skirts.

Reserved for Royalty

The color yellow was favored by emperors from different dynasties. During the Tang dynasty, only the royal family was allowed to wear this color. Emperors throughout the centuries also wore robes embroidered with **dragons**.

JEWELRY AND ACCESSORIES

Mulan's mother and grandmother help her prepare for the matchmaker. They give her a **jade** necklace, an apple, and even a lucky cricket!
The most important item Mulan receives is a flowered comb, a family **heirloom**.

Combs

Combs were a popular accessory in ancient China. Women wore them in their hair. The combs were often made of gold or jade. Jade is a hard stone that is usually green. It can also come in other colors like pink or white. In China, jade can be more precious than gold or silver.

Fans and Parasols

Some accessories were quite useful. People carried hand fans to cool themselves in hot weather. The fans were made from bamboo, silk, feathers, or paper. Foldable fans, brought to China from Japan, later became popular. **Parasols**, light umbrellas made of bamboo and paper, helped protect against the sun. Fans and parasols were often painted with elegant designs.

Other Accessories

Wealthy people might also wear bracelets, rings, hairpins, and **pendants**. Pendants are ornaments that can be worn on necklaces or sashes. Sometimes, they were attached to elaborate knots woven from cords. Jewelry often had designs with flowers or animals on them. These designs meant different things. For example, butterflies represented long life and the lotus flower represented purity.

HONORING THE ANCESTORS

The Fa family temple includes tablets representing all the **ancestors**. Mulan and her family honor the ancestors by visiting the **shrine** and keeping it clean. Sometimes, they pray for guidance and support before important events or decisions.

Showing Respect

Ancestors are family members from previous generations. Honoring one's ancestors has been an important part of Chinese culture for thousands of years. Wealthy families might build large temples devoted to their ancestors. Commoners might set up a small ancestral shrine inside their home.

Important Traditions

Honoring family members even after they pass away is one way to show filial piety. People regularly pray at their family shrine and make **offerings**. These may include food, drinks, and other gifts. It is believed that these offerings will help ancestors' spirits enjoy the afterlife.

Qingming Festival

The Qingming Festival is a holiday dedicated to remembering and honoring ancestors. The holiday, which takes place in early April, has been celebrated in China for over 2,500 years. On this day, families visit their ancestors' graves. They clean the graves and present special offerings. They also light scented sticks called **incense** and burn **joss paper**, which represents money.

JOINING THE ARMY

The arrival of the Emperor's men interrupts Mulan's time with her family. Chi Fu, the Emperor's adviser, gives each family a **conscription** scroll. One man from each family must serve in the Imperial Army.

Strict Rules

The order to join the army must be obeyed. Mulan's father is a war hero, but he was injured in battle. Worried that he won't survive another war, Mulan decides to go in his place. She cuts her hair, dresses in her father's armor, and rides off to the army camp. If anyone finds out she is female, her punishment is death. Ruling with strict laws and harsh punishments is a way of governing called **legalism**.

Military Dress

Ancient Chinese **armor** was made of leather, bronze, or iron. Armor helped protect soldiers from serious injuries in battle. The armor was layered like fish scales, which kept it from being too heavy. It also allowed soldiers to move more easily when they fought. Soldiers often wore helmets, too.

Eternal Warriors

The design of Mulan's armor was partly inspired by statues found in an ancient **tomb**. These **terra-cotta** warriors were made for the tomb of Qin Shi Huang. The Qin emperor wanted the life-size statues to serve as his army in the afterlife.

ARMY LIFE

When Mulan and the other recruits arrive at the army camp, they meet their captain. It is Captain Li Shang's job to train the recruits and make sure they're ready for battle.

Training

Most volunteer and conscripted soldiers didn't have any military experience. So they needed training. During the Han dynasty, new soldiers went through at least one year of training. Recruits trained in one of three groups: **infantry**, **cavalry**, or **navy**. Infantry soldiers trained for fighting on foot. Cavalry soldiers trained for fighting on horseback. Navy soldiers trained for fighting on ships.

Chinese Swords

Besides training to improve strength and discipline, soldiers learned to use weapons, including swords. There are two kinds of Chinese swords. The *jian* is a straight double-edged sword. This means the blade is sharp on both sides. The *dao* is a single-edged sword that may be straight or curved. The protective covering for swords is called a **scabbard**.

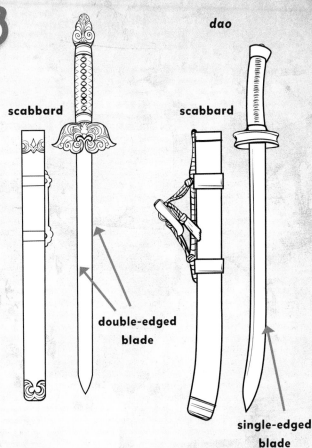

jian

dao

scabbard

scabbard

double-edged blade

single-edged blade

Other Weapons

Other weapons used in ancient China included spears, bows and arrows, long poles, and **crossbows**. A crossbow is a weapon with a short bow attached to a bar, usually made of wood. Crossbows are easier to use than bows and arrows. Look at this drawing of a Han dynasty battle. Can you find the crossbows?

ANIMAL SYMBOLS

Three animal companions help Mulan on her journey: Mushu the dragon, Khan the horse, and Cri-Kee the cricket. Different animals represent different qualities in Chinese culture. Let's learn about the traits associated with Mulan's animal friends.

Dragon

The dragon is a **symbol** of power and good fortune. Although Mushu breathes fire, Chinese dragons are traditionally associated with water. Throughout many dynasties, the dragon served as the symbol of the emperor.

Cricket

The cricket is a symbol of good harvest and good luck. During the Tang dynasty, it became popular to keep crickets in cages to enjoy their singing.

The horse symbolizes loyalty and strength. Horses were greatly valued because they served important roles on farms and during wars.

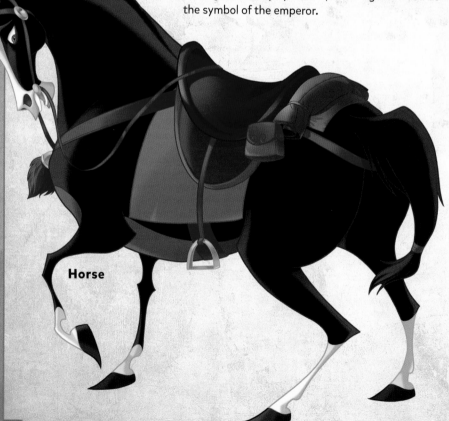

Horse

24

Chinese Zodiac

Traditional Chinese calendars are organized in twelve-year cycles, with a different animal representing each year. The animals are the rat, ox, tiger, rabbit, dragon, snake, horse, sheep, monkey, rooster, dog, and pig. This order of animals, known as the **Chinese zodiac**, repeats every twelve years.

Zodiac
Origins

An ancient myth explains how the Chinese zodiac came to be. The Jade Emperor wanted twelve animals to be his guards. He invited all animals to race to the Heavenly Gate. The first twelve to finish the race would be honored with a place in the twelve-year calendar. During the race, the ox helped carry the rat across a river. The clever rat jumped off the ox at the Heavenly Gate and earned first place. The order in which the animals finished the race determined their place in the calendar.

Chinese zodiac statues at a temple

FOOD AND DRINK

Mushu tries to make sure Mulan eats to keep up her strength. Through the difficult training, the soldiers miss the comforts of home. This includes delicious home-cooked meals.

Popular Foods

Commoners in ancient China ate mostly grains, vegetables, and fruits. Different regions grew different **crops**. People in the south ate rice. People in the north ate foods made from wheat, including noodles and dumplings. Chicken, pork, beef, or fish were eaten only on special occasions. The foods and recipes that developed in China over the centuries have become popular all around the world.

Tofu

Tofu is a type of curd made from mashed soybeans. The curd is pressed into soft white blocks to make tofu. The earliest record of tofu being made comes from the Han dynasty. Tofu itself doesn't have much flavor, so it can be prepared in many ways. Cooks might add soy sauce, ginger, garlic, and spices. Tofu can even be served as a sweet dessert!

Tea plant

Tea

Tea became a popular drink in China during the Tang and Song dynasties. Making tea involves several steps. First, farmers gather leaves from tea plants. Then they process the leaves. This often includes drying and then roasting or steaming the leaves. To prepare tea as a drink, you steep the processed leaves in boiling water.

CHINESE WRITING

Mushu thinks Mulan will become a hero if she proves herself in battle. He comes up with a plan. He and Cri-Kee sneak into Chi Fu's tent. There, they write a letter ordering Shang to lead the recruits into battle!

Chinese Characters

The Chinese system of writing has been in use for over 3,500 years. Instead of using an alphabet to spell words, the Chinese language uses symbols called **characters**. Chinese is written in columns. You read characters from top to bottom and columns from right to left. The language includes thousands of characters that people must memorize.

Object	Early Forms of Chinese		Modern Chinese	English
⛰	⛰	屮	山	mountain
🌳	人	朮	木	wood

Calligraphy

The art of handwriting in an elegant style is called **calligraphy**. The Chinese valued calligraphy as an important skill. In fact, during the Tang dynasty, calligraphy was one of the skills needed to get a government job. Today, Chinese calligraphy remains a respected art form.

Writing Tools

The Chinese use a brush and black ink to write calligraphy. To make the ink, calligraphers rub an **ink stick** with water on an **inkstone**. Then they dip the brush in the ink and write the words on paper or silk.

Chinese Seals

Works of calligraphy usually include one or more stamps in red ink. These stamps are made by putting red paste on a carved seal and applying the design to paper. Often, the stamp represents the writer's signature.

TRADITIONAL CHINESE ART

While working on the letter, Mushu notices a brush painting of Chi Fu with the Emperor. Chi Fu is very proud to be the Emperor's adviser!

Brush Painting

Traditional Chinese painting uses many of the same tools and techniques as calligraphy. Artists typically paint scenes from nature, such as mountains, trees, bamboo, and flowers. Harmony with nature is important in Chinese art. Paintings might include a poem or description written in calligraphy.

Ming dynasty painting

Porcelain

The Chinese invented **porcelain** during the Han dynasty. To make porcelain, artists heated clay and other materials to a high temperature. The process resulted in a strong material useful for making pottery, sculptures, and decorations. Artists might paint patterns and pictures on the porcelain before heating it. This kind of painting is called **enamel**.

Chinese porcelain

Enamel vase

Tang dynasty ceramic figure

Sculpture

You've already learned about the life-size sculptures in the Qin emperor's tomb. The ancient Chinese also created smaller figures using porcelain or other **ceramic** material. These sculptures might be used as decoration or put in tombs of important people.

CHINA'S GEOGRAPHY

Chi Fu and Li Shang think Mushu's letter came from the general. The soldiers travel toward the mountains in northern China, ready to join the battle. Along the way, they encounter mountains, plains, rivers, and farmlands.

Diverse Terrains

China has many different **terrains**. This means the features of its land can differ greatly from region to region. The country contains mountains, deserts, forests, grasslands, lakes, and rivers. The Yangtze River, the third-longest river in the world, flows from China's western mountains to the Pacific Ocean.

Yangtze River

Working with the Land

To live and grow food in certain terrains, people sometimes modified the land. One example is cutting flat areas in hillsides so the land can be farmed. These areas look like steps and are called terraces.

Terraced rice fields

Animals and Plants

China's different terrains and **climates** make it possible for many different animals and plants to live there. In fact, China has over thirty thousand unique species of animals and plants. Species that are **endemic** to China do not naturally live or grow anywhere else in the world.

Chinese flowering chestnut

Ginkgo biloba tree

Giant Panda

Golden snub-nosed monkey

CHINESE INVENTIONS

During the battle with Shan-Yu and his army, Mulan uses a cannon to start an avalanche. The rocket cannon is one of many advanced technologies invented in China.

Explosive Discoveries

The Chinese invented firecrackers early in the Han dynasty. They discovered that leaving bamboo on a fire caused it to explode with a loud sound. People would light firecrackers to scare off evil spirits. During the Tang dynasty, the Chinese created **gunpowder**. The first fireworks were made by putting gunpowder into bamboo stalks and throwing them on a fire. Over the next centuries, the Chinese developed the technology to fire explosives into the air. They used weapons like the rocket cannon in battle. Fireworks that created pretty explosions in the sky were used in celebrations.

Kite

The Chinese invented kites over two thousand years ago. They used bamboo for the frames and silk for the fabric. Flying kites became a popular activity, but did you know that kites were also a useful tool? Written records show that the Chinese used kites to send messages, measure distances, and test the wind.

Compass

The first **compass** was invented during the Han dynasty. It used a magnetized rock called a **lodestone**. This compass design included a bronze plate with a spoon carved from lodestone. The spoon would spin and stop when the handle pointed south. Several hundred years later, the Chinese developed the needle compass for navigating at sea.

Earthquake Detector

A Han dynasty **astronomer** named Zhang Heng invented the first earthquake detector. The device showed which direction an earthquake was coming from. It could detect an earthquake from over 600 miles (1,000 km) away.

MUSIC AND DANCE

Shang and his soldiers march to the Imperial capital, thinking they've defeated the Huns. People celebrate in the streets with music and dance.

Ancient drum tower

Chinese chime bells

Drums and Bells

Drums and bells have a rich history in China. Drums came in lots of different sizes and materials. People beat on drums during celebrations and festivals. The army also used drums during battle to motivate soldiers and help them work together. Metal bells were used in religious ceremonies and at the emperor's court. Chime bells consisted of a set of bronze bells hung in a wooden frame. Each bell played a different note when struck with a mallet.

Other Instruments

The oldest musical instruments discovered in China are flutes made from bone. These bone flutes are over eight thousand years old! Over time, the Chinese developed a variety of flutes, usually made from bamboo. Another important instrument in traditional music is the Chinese **zither**. Musicians play the zither by plucking its strings.

Bamboo flute

Chinese zither

Traditional Dance

Dance has been an art in China for over two thousand years. Originally, dances were performed during special ceremonies. Later on, dancing became popular for entertainment and at festivals. A famous traditional dance is the **dragon dance**. Dancers would dress as dragons and dance to ask for rain from the gods. Today, people perform this dance at celebrations and festivals. Multiple dancers hold a long dragon costume, creating movements that resemble flowing water.

Modern dragon dance

MARTIAL ARTS

Shan-Yu survives the battle in the mountains. He sneaks into the Imperial Palace and tries to capture the Emperor. With cleverness, courage, and skill, Mulan defeats Shan-Yu in this final fight.

Kung Fu

The arts of fighting and self-defense are called **martial arts**. People often use the term **kung fu** to refer to Chinese martial arts. Kung fu dates back over 2,500 years. At first, kung fu skills focused on fighting without weapons. By the Han dynasty, kung fu had evolved to include fighting with swords, wooden poles, and spears.

Monks and Martial Arts

One of the most famous styles of kung fu is Shaolin kung fu. It is named for a **monastery** located in Henan, China. The Shaolin **monks** followed a religion called **Buddhism**. To protect their temple, many of the monks learned kung fu. The warrior monks developed many new fighting techniques. Shaolin kung fu strongly influenced much of the Chinese martial arts we see today.

Shaolin temple

Demonstration of Shaolin kung fu

Fighting Fans

During Mulan's fight with Shan-Yu, she uses her fan to twist away his sword. Some forms of Chinese martial arts incorporate the use of fans. Fans designed for fighting were foldable and made of metal or wood. The ends of the fan were sharp, making it a dangerous weapon. Eventually, movements from fighting with fans inspired fan dances.

CELEBRATIONS AND FESTIVALS

After Shan-Yu's defeat, Mulan is honored by the Emperor. The people cheer, and the celebration continues with lanterns, fireworks, and music.

Traditional Holidays

Lanterns, fireworks, and music play an important role in many holiday celebrations. Traditionally, the Chinese people use a calendar based on the cycles of the moon and the sun. The Chinese calendar is often called a **lunar calendar**. This is because "lunar" means related to the moon. Here are some important traditional Chinese holidays.

Holiday	Time of Year	Purpose
Chinese New Year	January 1 (lunar calendar)	Celebrates the new year and the coming of spring
Lantern Festival	January 15 (lunar calendar)	Celebrates the first full moon of the new year
Qingming Festival	early spring	Honors ancestors
Dragon Boat Festival	May 5 (lunar calendar)	Honors an ancient poet
Mid-Autumn Festival	August 15 (lunar calendar)	Celebrates the harvest

Chinese New Year

Chinese New Year is celebrated on the first new moon of the lunar calendar. The holiday usually lands between January 21 and February 20 on the Gregorian calendar. Families celebrate Chinese New Year for many days. They wear red clothing and have family dinners. They also give red envelopes filled with money to children. Red is considered a lucky color in China.

Dragon Boat Festival

The Dragon Boat Festival takes place in the summer. It honors Qu Yuan, a famous poet who was also a government official. Popular traditions include racing boats decorated to look like dragons and eating **zongzi**. This is a dumpling made with rice and fillings and wrapped in bamboo leaves.

Mid-Autumn Festival

The Chinese celebrate the Mid-Autumn Festival during the fall. It is a time where families gather and give thanks for a good harvest. They enjoy watching the full moon and eating moon cakes.

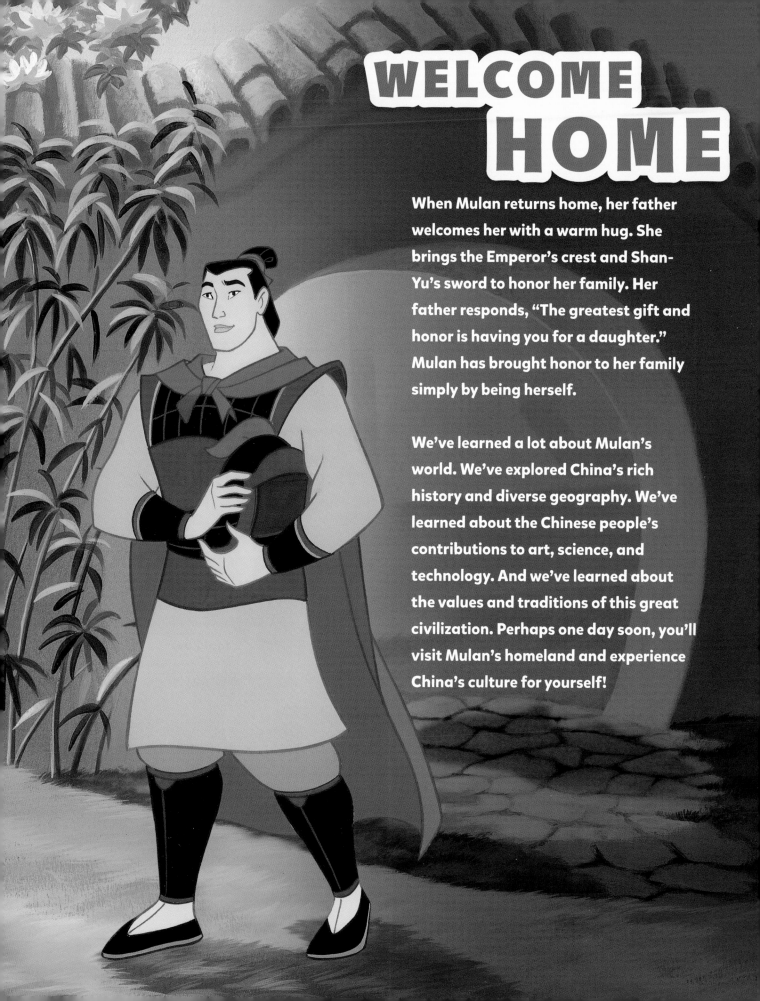

WELCOME HOME

When Mulan returns home, her father welcomes her with a warm hug. She brings the Emperor's crest and Shan-Yu's sword to honor her family. Her father responds, "The greatest gift and honor is having you for a daughter." Mulan has brought honor to her family simply by being herself.

We've learned a lot about Mulan's world. We've explored China's rich history and diverse geography. We've learned about the Chinese people's contributions to art, science, and technology. And we've learned about the values and traditions of this great civilization. Perhaps one day soon, you'll visit Mulan's homeland and experience China's culture for yourself!

GLOSSARY

ancestor: a family member from an older generation

armor: protective clothing for soldiers, usually made of leather, bronze, or iron

Asia: a continent mainly located in the Northern and Eastern Hemispheres

astronomer: someone who studies stars, planets, and other objects seen in the night sky

Before the Common Era (BCE): the notation for dates before year 1 CE on the Gregorian calendar

Buddhism: a religion that originated in India and spread to other parts of the world, including China

calligraphy: the art of handwriting in an elegant style

capital: the city where a country's government is based

cavalry: soldiers who fight on horseback

ceramic: made by heating clay and other materials to a high temperature

character: a symbol used in the written Chinese language to represent an object or idea

China: a large country located in Asia with one of the world's oldest civilizations

Chinese zodiac: the twelve-year cycle in traditional Chinese calendars in which each year is represented by an animal

civilization: a people who live in a region over a long period of time, developing unique traditions and practices

climate: weather conditions and patterns in a region

Common Era (CE): the notation for dates in the modern era, starting at year 1 CE on the Gregorian calendar

compass: a device that helps determine directions

Confucianism: a belief system based on the teachings of Confucius

conscription: an official order stating that citizens must join the army for a period of time

crop: a plant that people grow to use or sell

crossbow: a weapon with a short bow attached to a bar that fires bolts when the trigger is pulled

culture: a people's beliefs, values, traditions, and achievements

dragon: a mythical flying animal that is a symbol of power and good fortune in China

dragon dance: a traditional Chinese dance where multiple dancers dress up as a dragon and perform as part of rituals or celebrations

dynasty: a family that ruled ancient China for multiple generations

emperor: the ruler of a large region of land and all the people who live there

enamel: a paint that is added to pottery and sculptures that leaves a glossy texture

endemic: naturally existing in only one location

filial piety: the practice of respecting and obeying parents' and grandparents' wishes

garrison: a station where soldiers stay to watch over and guard an area

Great Wall: an extensive wall built to protect China's northern borders from invaders

Gregorian calendar: the calendar most widely used in the world today

gunpowder: a powder made from a mixture of ingredients that can cause an explosion when lit

Hanfu: the traditional style of Chinese clothing

heirloom: a valuable object passed down from one generation to the next

honor: a family's good reputation that is respected by the community

incense: scented sticks that are burned when praying to gods or ancestors

infantry: soldiers who fight on foot

ink stick: solid ink shaped into a stick. When ground with water on an inkstone, it produces ink for writing and painting

inkstone: a hard dish made for for grinding and holding ink

jade: a hard gemstone that is usually green

joss paper: paper meant to represent money that is burned to honor ancestors

kung fu: a style of Chinese martial arts

legalism: governing with strict laws and harsh punishments

lodestone: a type of magnetized rock

lunar calendar: a calendar based on the cycle of the moon's phases

martial arts: the arts of fighting and self-defense

monastery: a place where people who have taken religious vows live

monk: someone who has taken a religious vow and lives in a monastery

navy: ships and soldiers who fight in water battles

nomadic: moving about regularly from place to place

offering: something presented to ancestors or gods as part of a ceremony

parasol: a small and light umbrella used to protect against the sun

parliament: the part of a country's government responsible for making laws and representing the people

pendant: an ornament that can be worn on a necklace or hanging from a sash

porcelain: a strong, usually white material used to make pottery, sculptures, and decorations

scabbard: a protective covering for a sword

shrine: a place set up to pay respects and make offerings to gods or ancestors

silk: a soft, light fabric made from the cocoons of silkworms

Silk Road: routes that helped China trade silk, tea, and other items for goods from Central Asian and some European countries

socialize: to talk and visit with members of the community

symbol: something that represents an idea or quality

tea: a drink made from steeping processed leaves from tea plants in boiling water

terra-cotta: a type of clay heated by fire to create statues, pottery, and building materials

terrain: the features of the land

tofu: a type of curd made from mashed soybeans

tomb: a place, often underground, built to bury the dead

watchtower: a tower, built for defensive purposes, that provides views of the surrounding areas

zither: a type of instrument made of many strings that are stretched and then plucked to play different notes

zongzi: a dumpling made with rice and fillings and wrapped in bamboo leaves

INDEX

bamboo, 17, 30, 34–35, 37, 41

Beijing, 10–11

brush painting, 30

Buddhism, 39

calligraphy, 29–30

Chinese New Year, 40–41

Chinese writing, 28–29

Chinese zodiac, 25

civilization, 4

compasses, 35

Confucianism, 13

Confucius, 13

Dragon Boat Festival, 40–41

dragon dance, 37

dragons, 15, 24–25, 37

earthquake detectors, 35

fans, 17, 39

filial piety, 13, 19

firecrackers, 34

fireworks, 34

Forbidden City, 11

Four Great Ancient Capitals, 10

Giant Wild Goose Pagoda, 10

golden snub-nosed monkey, 33

Great Wall, 8–9

Gregorian calendar, 6, 41

gunpowder, 7, 34

Han dynasty, 6–7, 10, 13–14, 22–23, 27, 31, 34–35, 38

Hanfu, 14–15

inventions, 4, 7, 34–35

jade, 16

kites, 35

kung fu, 38–39

legalism, 20

lunar calendar, 40

Luoyang, 10

martial arts, 38–39

Mid-Autumn Festival, 40–41

Ming dynasty, 6, 9, 30

Nanjing, 10

pandas, 33

paper, 7, 17, 29

poetry, 5, 7, 30

population, 4

porcelain, 7, 31

Qin dynasty, 6, 9, 21, 31

Qin Shi Huang, 9, 21, 31

Qing dynasty, 6, 11

Qingming Festival, 19, 40

Qu Yuan, 40–41

rocket cannons, 34

Shaolin, 39

silk, 7, 15, 17, 29, 35

Silk Road, 7

swords, 23, 38

Tang dynasty, 6–7, 10, 15, 24, 27, 29, 31, 34

tea, 7, 27

terra-cotta warriors, 21

tofu, 27

White Horse Temple, 10

Xi'an, 10

Yangtze River, 32

Zhang Heng, 35

zither, 37

PHOTO CREDITS

All photos are listed by page number from top to bottom.